RESEARCH IN POLITICAL SCIENCE

an SSRC review of current research

SOCIAL SCIENCE RESEARCH COUNCIL

Reviews of current research

1. Research in Political Science
2. Research on International Organization
3. Research in Social Anthropology
4. Research on Automation

Research in Political Science

HEINEMANN
LONDON

Heinemann Educational Books Ltd
LONDON MELBOURNE TORONTO
SINGAPORE JOHANNESBURG
AUCKLAND IBADAN
NAIROBI

First published 1968

SBN 435 82840 1

Published by Heinemann Educational Books Ltd
48 Charles Street, London W.1
for the Social Science Research Council,
State House, High Holborn, London W.C.1
Printed in Great Britain by
Cox & Wyman Ltd,
London, Fakenham and Reading

Contents

FOREWORD   vi

INTRODUCTION   vii

MEMBERSHIP OF SSRC POLITICAL SCIENCE
COMMITTEE   viii

1. *Some definitions*   1

2. *Political Science in Britain*   3
   The universities
   The Members of the Political Studies Association
   The institutes
   Summary of fields and trends

3. *Topics in British political science*   17
   Classification
   Political Theory
   British Government
   Comparative Politics
   International Relations
   Controversial innovations

4. *Objects to be achieved*   50

5. *Resources required*   55
   Help to individuals
   General facilities
   Research overseas

Foreword

JEREMY MITCHELL, *series editor*

This is one of a series of reviews, prepared under the auspices of the Social Science Research Council (SSRC), which deals with various aspects of research in the social sciences.

One of the SSRC's main reasons for sponsoring the preparation of these reviews is to get the views of some of the leading research workers in the field about important current research developments, about likely future developments and about the research needs of the subject, in terms of men, money, other resources and research organization.

As well as helping to guide the SSRC in its future policy, the research reviews will, at a time when there is increasing specialization within all social science disciplines, help social scientists and students to keep abreast of developments over a wider field.

The reviews will also provide those in industry, government, the educational world and elsewhere with information about recent developments in the social sciences.

The research reviews are prepared in different ways. Some are drawn up by Committees of the Council, others by *ad hoc* panels of specialists brought together with the sole aim of compiling a review. Some deal with a particular social science discipline, others with a problem or range of problems involving a number of disciplines. The reviews do not therefore follow any standardized pattern, and the groups involved in preparing them are free to tackle them in whatever ways they think are appropriate.

Some social science disciplines and problems may not be susceptible to this kind of approach, and so this series of reviews does not aim to provide a comprehensive picture of everything that is going on in all the social sciences. It should also be stressed that the reviews are in no sense formal policy statements by the SSRC – their function is to inform.

Introduction

This research report needs only a brief introduction.

First, it should be made clear to general readers that the report was conceived not as a piece of research but as part of a process of consultation. It is concerned primarily with the interests and needs of those who research and teach in this field in the United Kingdom; and it has been the basis of a number of specific recommendations to the SSRC which are not included here.

Second, the Committee assume joint responsibility for these recommendations but not for all the arguments and phraseology of the report. They gave a very free hand to James Cornford for the inquiry among members of the Political Studies Association, to Professor Geoffrey Goodwin for the drafting of the section on International Relations (Chapter 3), and to myself for the remainder of Chapters 1–5. The Committee exercised vigorously the right to be consulted, to advise and to warn; but those of us who did the drafting are grateful to them for recognizing that a Committee cannot draft.

Third, we realized, as correspondence with foreign schools developed, that our report was concerned with a small part of a world-wide debate about the place of the social sciences in relation to politics. We are indebted to many scholars in other countries for personal letters and for documents relating to their own parallel inquiries.

W. J. M. MACKENZIE

MEMBERSHIP OF SSRC POLITICAL SCIENCE COMMITTEE

1. Some definitions

There are various disputes about the scope and methods (and even about the name) of political science; these need only a brief reference here.

The oldest and most convenient definition limits the scope of the subject to discussion of 'polities', their internal structure and their external relations; a polity in this sense being in each age of history that authority which makes good a claim to external independence and to legitimate rule within its own borders. But this approach involves us at once in legal, philosophical, and practical puzzles about the nature of sovereignty, and attempts are made to escape these puzzles by defining 'politics' as some aspect of all human groups and communities which persist for some time. The study of politics would thus be one aspect of the study of society, and would include political psychology, political sociology, geo-politics, and so on. There are, however, a good many different ways of specifying what this political aspect is.

As regards methods, it would probably be agreed that the discipline has no special axioms or techniques of its own. There are certainly a number of words and phrases, such as 'power', 'authority', 'leadership', 'freedom', 'consent', 'justice', 'rights', which are prominent in serious political discussion. But these terms are not defined in a way independent of the natural languages in which they occur, and they are not linked to form an agreed axiomatic structure, as is for instance the terminology of classical economics. The structure of political argument is complex and manifold; similarly, the methods of study are chosen from the common stock of techniques available at the time. Traditionally, the most common techniques have been those of law, philosophy, and history; but for at least the last fifty years there has been a growing tendency to adopt mathematical analogies (cybernetics, games theory, information theory, and so on), and to use the statistical techniques which have become the common tools of the social sciences.

The term 'political science' was established in regular use in England in the middle of the nineteenth century, when the word 'science' corresponded more closely than it does now to the French *science* or German *Wissenschaft*, words applicable to any organized and disciplined field of inquiry. Some of those who are not familiar with this usage take 'political science' to imply a commitment to the use of 'scientific' methods in political study, and they associate science closely with mathematics and with measurement. On the whole, we find it most convenient to use the term 'political science', which seems clearer than the use of words such as 'politics', 'political studies', or 'government'. But this is not intended to suggest that a line can be drawn between the 'humanistic' and the 'scientific' study of politics. In the 1940s and 1950s there was a good deal of controversy in the USA about 'the scientific study of political behaviour', and the work done by the American 'behaviourists' has been influential in the UK. But the controversy about method was not taken very seriously in Britain, and it has died down now even in the USA. There are many different forms of political study, and specialization is increasing: but there is little disposition to claim that there is 'one best way', and one only.

2. Political Science in Britain

The universities

Organized university teaching in Western countries has always included some study of politics, but the present tradition in England had its origin in the 1840s and 1850s, when the study of Plato's *Republic* and Aristotle's *Politics* revived in Oxford, and 'political economy' became an examination subject, particularly in the University of London. Political science shared in the advance of the social sciences in the years just before 1914, and chairs were founded then at the London School of Economics and in Oxford. A chair was added at Cambridge in 1927, but the most notable development between the wars was the emergence of the study of international relations in the universities, notably in London, at Oxford and at Aberystwyth. This happened partly because dramatic developments in foreign affairs attracted benefactors, and this led in particular to the establishment of the Royal Institute of International Affairs. But intellectual issues were equally involved, in that political science had till then been concerned primarily with the problems of sovereign states, not with those of the international system, and had drawn on a relatively limited range of sources and disciplines. Teaching and research in international relations brought something new to the academic study of politics.

At one time it seemed that these branches of study might diverge, but probably that time is now past. Political science has expanded its scope; indeed, the importance of international relations is now so great that it has to be included in some form in any course of teaching about politics. In addition, politics teaching now takes greater cognizance of the social sciences as a whole, and emphasizes the interrelation of politics, economics, culture, and social structure, within states and between states. In consequence, international relations is in many universities combined with politics in a single department, and the most common practice now is to treat it as one of the most important parts of political science rather than as a separate discipline. It is quite common to find lecturers who contribute to teaching both in politics and in international relations, and it is not always possible to show international relations separately in the statistics in the next section.

Members of the Political Studies Association
In reporting on trends and priorities in research, we have drawn on our own knowledge and experience, and also on consultation with a number of distinguished foreign scholars. We realized, however, that there had in recent years been a very rapid increase in the number of political scientists teaching in British universities, as is reflected by the figures in Table 1 below, and that it was important to learn as much as we could about the needs and problems of these scholars, who are on the whole relatively young (Table 2). With this in mind, we sent a brief questionnaire to all members of the Political Studies Association of the United Kingdom, and we are grateful to them for the help they gave us. We could not in the time available design a proper piece of research, and our questionnaire was rather informal. But it has, for the first time, provided us with figures to indicate the scale of the problem; and we have also been able to draw on a great many replies to 'open-ended' questions about research work planned and in progress, and the difficulties met.

TABLE 1

MEMBERSHIP OF THE POLITICAL STUDIES ASSOCIATION
OF THE UK

(*Source:* PSA data)

1951	–	100 (actual)	1961	–	197
1953	–	122	1962	–	221
1954	–	126	1963	–	231
1955	–	142	1964	–	259
1956	–	152	1965	–	270
1958	–	163	1966	–	352
1959	–	177	1967	–	400
1960	–	179	Jan. 1968	–	442

The Political Studies Association of the United Kingdom was founded in 1950, and in its first complete year it had 100 members; this figure itself represented a rapid increase during the post-war expansion of the universities, and was at least double the number that could have been attained in 1939. Table 1 shows the rate of build-up to 1968; membership of the PSA is limited to the staff of universities and research institutes in Britain, Ireland, and overseas, and to the staff of other colleges if they have had some research experience and teach a fair number of students to final honours degree standard. Out of 442 members over 400 are now teaching in British universities.

Table 2 is based on returns to our inquiry; there were 301 replies, but not all were complete, and the totals shown in this and other tables do not coincide. For this and other reasons we think it fairer to show the data as we received them rather than to attempt statistical analysis. It is easy to see the predominance of the lower age-groups; and this is related to the startling increase of PSA membership, from 270 in 1965 to 352 in 1966. We have no data about length of service in universities, but we know of many cases of transfer to universities after previous experience in other relevant fields (Foreign Service, colonial service, local government and so on). Probably the 35–44 age-group includes a number of people of this kind, who bring valuable qualities and experience, but still have a good deal to learn about university teaching and research.

This table also shows how the emphasis changes with the generations. Out of 78 members aged 45 or over 23 held a first degree with a strong element of political science in it. Out of 216 younger members, 122 had such a degree. The trend is towards self-perpetuation in the discipline, but boundaries are not rigid even now.

TABLE 2

SUBJECT OF FIRST DEGREE

(*Source*: PSA membership inquiry)

Subject	65+	55–64	45–54	35–44	25–34	24–	No indication of age	Totals
Politics, Govt.	–	2	10	33	44	8	1	98
Philosophy, Politics, and Economics (Oxford)	–	5	6	20	14	3	1	49
History	2	4	25	22	36	2	1	92
Classics	1	1	3	–	1	–	–	6
Philosophy	–	1	1	3	3	1	–	9
Economics	–	–	5	1	5	–	–	11
Sociology	1	2	2	3	4	2	–	14
Modern Languages	–	1	–	2	1	–	–	4
Law	–	2	3	1	4	–	–	10
Anthropology	–	–	–	1	–	–	–	1
Other	–	–	–	–	1	–	–	1
No indication	–	–	1	1	–	–	–	2
TOTAL	4	18	56	87	113	16	3	297

Table 3 compares age structure with university of first

degree, and shows the dominance of Oxford, Cambridge, and London. Apart from these, only Manchester has some strength in depth, but it is clear that in recent years universities outside 'the metropolitan triangle' have begun to be an important source of recruitment in total, and that there is a useful intake from the Commonwealth and from foreign countries.

TABLE 3

UNIVERSITY OF FIRST DEGREE

(*Source:* PSA membership inquiry)

University	65+	55–64	45–54	35–44	25–34	24–	No indication of age	Totals
Oxford	1	7	22	27	24	4	2	87
Cambridge	1	4	10	9	23	1	–	48
London	1	3	12	28	20	3	1	68
Manchester	1	1	–	1	2	–	–	5
Other English Provincial	–	–	1	5	20	4	–	30
English New	–	–	–	–	4	–	–	4
Wales	–	–	2	5	2	2	–	11
Scotland	–	–	–	4	6	1	–	11
Commonwealth and South Africa	–	–	3	2	3	1	–	9
USA	–	–	1	2	6	–	–	9
European	–	3	1	3	–	–	–	7
Dublin and Belfast	–	–	2	1	2	–	–	5
No indication	–	–	1	–	1	–	–	2
TOTAL	4	18	55	87	113	16	3	296

Table 4, relating to postgraduate work, shows a similar picture. Probably about a fifth of our respondents had no experience as graduate students. The position of Manchester shows up clearly, as does the importance of the USA, as regards graduate work. We have no figures to show how many students went to the USA for graduate work and did not return; nor have we any figures for the substantial export of graduates to universities in the Commonwealth, where expansion has been even more rapid than in the UK.

TABLE 4

UNIVERSITY OF POSTGRADUATE WORK

(*Note:* Respondents who did graduate work in two universities appear twice)

(*Source:* PSA membership inquiry)

University	65+	55–64	45–54	35–44	25–34	24–	No indica-tion of age	Totals
Oxford	–	3	11	25	23	2	1	65
Cambridge	1	2	6	5	16	2	–	32
London	1	1	13	24	22	5	1	67
Manchester	–	2	1	3	9	–	–	15
Other English Provincial	–	2	–	7	6	3	–	18
English New	–	–	–	–	3	–	–	3
Wales	–	–	2	2	3	1	–	8
Scotland	–	–	–	3	1	–	–	4
Commonwealth and South Africa	–	–	1	–	5	–	–	6
USA	1	1	4	7	10	–	–	23
European	–	1	–	1	3	–	–	5
Dublin and Belfast	–	–	2	–	–	–	–	2
None	1	6	16	13	15	3	1	55
TOTAL	4	18	56	90	116	16	3	303

Table 5 gives the best indication we can get of the interests of our respondents and of present trends. It is not of course inevitable that a man should work later in the field he has chosen as a graduate student: but the figures suggest that the historical and philosophical approaches are still strong, that the main concentration is on the traditional study of Parliament, parties, elections, and other aspects of the constitution, and that 'behavioural' or sociological studies are exceptional. International relations seems to have been growing more rapidly than any other field; but our data about relative rates of growth are incomplete, as some 'behavioural' studies of politics originate in departments of sociology and social psychology, and some of the work of history departments and law departments (not included in our PSA survey) is relevant to politics, including international relations.

TABLE 5

SUBJECT OF POSTGRADUATE WORK

(*Source:* PSA membership inquiry)

Subject	65+	55–64	45–54	Age 35–44	25–34	24–	No indica- tion of age	Totals
Political Thought[1]	–	1	2	5	11	2	–	21
Political Theory[1]	1	1	3	5	3	–	–	13
History	3	2	8	16	26	1	–	56
Local Govt.	–	–	1	2	4	2	1	10
Parliament, Parties, Elections, etc.	–	5	5	25	33	3	1	72
Pub. Admin.	–	2	6	6	3	–	–	17
Int. Relations	–	–	2	3	8	5	–	18
Political Sociology	–	–	–	–	3	–	–	3
Psychology	–	–	–	1	–	–	–	1
Economics	–	1	3	2	2	–	–	8
Philosophy	–	–	3	2	–	–	–	5
Other	–	–	6	8	6	–	–	20
None	–	6	16	13	14	3	1	53
TOTAL	4	18	55	88	113	16	3	297

[1] By Political Thought is meant here the study of particular political theorists – or *Dogmengeschichte* – i.e. works on Plato or Locke or Hume and so forth, and by Political Theory works such as Weidon's *States and Morals*, contemporary essays on political philosophy and the methodology of political science.

The institutes

It is impossible to discuss the progress and resources of political research in Britain without some reference to institutes and other bodies with specialized functions. But the topic is a very complex one (indeed it is itself an unexplored field for research, as an aspect of the policy-making process in Britain), and it is possible here only to make some general points in a provisional way.

Three main areas can be distinguished, within a continuous spectrum.

First, there is the development of specialized institutes within the universities or annexed to them. Some of these were created by universities unprompted: for instance, the Institute of Soviet and East European Studies at Glasgow, and the Institute of Commonwealth Studies in London. Others arose out of the recommendations of the Scarbrough, Hayter, and Parry Committees, covering Soviet and East European studies, Oriental and African studies, and the study of Latin America. These institutes raise in particular the problem of 'political studies' in relation to 'area studies'. The Institutes of Local Government Studies at the Universities of Birmingham and Strathclyde were created on the initiative of these universities, but will depend for success on collaboration and financial support from other public bodies.

All these institutes are in part dependent on University Grants Committee (UGC) funds. They also draw funds from other sources, but they have not raised any academic or administrative problems distinct from those of university departments.

Secondly, there are institutes which are legally and financially independent of universities. These also are a miscellaneous group, each of them created and sustained individually to fill a particular niche in the ecology of political and social research. We cannot here give an adequate account of each of them, and it may be more valuable to attempt a summary of the general contribution of such institutes to research. This has three aspects:

First, the earliest relevant institutes, The Royal Institute of International Affairs (Chatham House), the Royal Institute of Public Administration (RIPA), and Political and Economic Planning (PEP), were founded when universities were more reluctant than they are now to engage in what is sometimes called 'policy research'. The distinction between 'academic' research and 'policy' research is not very clear in the social sciences, but it is perhaps more serviceable than that between 'pure' and 'applied' research. The problem is that of bringing the best available resources of academic and practical skill to bear on issues of urgent public importance; and the problem has generated its own techniques of consultation and collaboration between government, business, and the academic world. A number of universities (including Manchester, Glasgow, and London) helped to develop these techniques, and it is now as acceptable in this country as it is in the USA that universities should take the initiative in harnessing their resources to the solution of administrative, social, and economic problems. But institutes such as Chatham House, the RIPA and PEP still have a freedom of action rare in universities; and in addition these independent institutes, being established in London, are well placed to act as central points of contact between people active in different spheres.

Second, it is characteristic of research of this kind that the boundaries between academic disciplines are not important to it. So far as concerns political science as an academic discipline, the large contributions of the institutes have been in the spheres of international relations and of administrative institutions. These are areas of investigation in which politics plays a large but not dominant part; progress is made by

11

relating political to economic and social factors, and by making a 'best guess' on the basis of a common fund of practical experience and academic knowledge. We regard this as a very important kind of political thinking, and in that sense as part of our subject matter: but the essence of the technique is to avoid areas of profound theoretical controversy and to elicit a consensus between academics and practitioners in various fields about what should be done in the medium term. The scope of the inquiry is not that of the pure academic, nor yet that of the administrator who must clear his desk each day.

Third, there are facilities provided by the institutes which are essential to academic students as well as to practitioners.

They sponsor a number of journals which are indispensable in their several fields. *International Affairs* (Chatham House, which also produces *The World Today*) and *Public Administration* (RIPA) are the leading general periodicals for these fields in the UK. *Race* (the Institute of Race Relations), *Survival* (the Institute of Strategic Studies) and *Planning* (PEP) are not quite so central, but are nevertheless very useful indeed.

They also provide libraries and bibliographical services which are important to all research students, and which serve as a point of reference and enquiry for overseas visitors. Certainly the most valuable of these libraries is that of Chatham House, and its maintenance is of great general importance. But each institute serves as a central point of reference in any preliminary search directed to bibliographical sources and research in progress.

Several institutes provide press-cutting services in their own fields, but the biggest and most important of these is that at Chatham House. Indeed, Chatham House have in general gone further than other institutes in attracting endowment income and in applying it to provide services for the academic community and for other members of the public. Given the gradual but persistent increase in costs, this poses a problem to Chatham House and (on a smaller scale) to other institutes. One of their most important functions is to provide background information in specific fields, something which university libraries, even the libraries of university institutes, cannot do well. But the increasing cost of these services cuts into the endowment revenue available, and to that extent restricts the institute's power to innovate and to cross boundaries in inquiry, an equally valuable service.

Finally, there are the research activities of institutes of a professional kind. In this field, the most notable contribution has been that of the Institute of Municipal Treasurers and Accountants, which has sponsored a number of important research projects in the field of local government finance, and which also provides useful information services. Each professional body goes its own way, and no generalizations are possible: but enquiries sponsored from within the administrative professions may be of particular value because they afford access to the best sources of administrative information.

Some data are available about the finance and staffing of the eight institutes to which inquiries were sent, but the figures cannot be added together and summarized in tables. Probably, as the universities have expanded, the proportion of academic staff employed by institutes has declined relatively, but not absolutely. Institute appointments have in the past been held for relatively short periods, and this has fitted in well with the university system. Junior appointments in institutes have in fact served to give graduate training in research to a number of those now teaching in universities; and appointments at a more senior level are often filled by collaboration with universities, either by secondment or by part-time collaboration. There has also been some collaboration with the public services in regard to research appointments, but more could be done to develop interchangeability, which is of particular importance for the sort of work which is the staple of institute business.

Summary of fields and trends

In attempting to summarize 'the state of the art' in the UK we pay particular attention to work in universities: this does not mean that the work of the institutes can be set on one side. So far as the universities are concerned, there has been an explosive expansion in the last ten years in the scale of teaching and research in political science, and this has been accompanied by some changes in the pattern of recruitment and of interests. This pattern cannot be defined precisely, and it is changing continually. Nevertheless, it is perhaps possible to define a 'main stream' in very general terms, and then to indicate divergent trends.

The 'main stream' is related to a system of teaching which combines detailed analysis of certain classics of political thought with descriptive study of one or more polities. The analysis of great books is sometimes philosophical in style, sometimes historical; and the elements of descriptive politics may be compounded of law, history, and contemporary observation in varying proportions. Bagehot (*Physics and Politics*, 1872) and Graham Wallas (*Human Nature in Politics*, 1908) were pioneers in harnessing sociology and social psychology to the study of politics, and this also is part of the tradition. But 'main-stream' political scientists have been relatively slow to adopt the 'tools of social science' (the title of John Madge's book[1]). Their methods have been those

---

[1] J. Madge, *The Tools of Social Science* (Longmans, London, 1953).

traditional in humane scholarship, and they have in general been 'problem-oriented', not 'discipline-oriented'; that is to say, they have in general tackled issues of theory, analysis, and recommendation as they arise, and have not set out to establish empirically a body of truths about politics in general. The tradition recognizes the recurrence of similar problems in different settings, and ventures some generalizations about them; indeed, it relies much both on history in general, and on sociology and social psychology in general. But it lays more emphasis on analysis than on generalization, and it sees no harm in making recommendations, provided that their basis is clearly set out.

It is tempting to say that this attitude is 'typically English', but in fact it is strong also in the USA, though it attracts less notice there than does the behavioural movement. It is also strong in the Commonwealth countries: but in Western Europe the 'main stream' has been more strongly legal, sociological, and philosophical in character.

This tradition is attacked from two flanks, in ways which should not be identified as either 'progressive' or 'reactionary'. Both of them are radical, in the sense that they proclaim radical intellectual dissatisfaction with the present state of affairs. It is argued (on the one hand) that in so far as it makes recommendations political science is not a truly academic subject, and that if this is taken away there is nothing left which is not the subject of other disciplines. On the other hand, there have always been voices (Professor G. E. G. Catlin is the elder statesman of this trend in England, and was in fact ahead of the Americans in proclaiming it[1]) which cry for a complete renewal of concepts and techniques so as to establish for the first time a true science of politics. This science, they

---

[1] G. E. G. Catlin, *The Science and Method of Politics* (London, 1926, rep. Shoestring Press, Connecticut, 1964).

would say, *must* be found, because ignorance of it is the source of great danger to all men; and they would refer to the enormous power of the procedures used by the natural sciences. Political science, as they define it, would be one of the natural sciences of mankind; indeed it might lose its separate identity within the complex of behavioural sciences.

Of these two radical trends, perhaps the former is the stronger in the UK; but it is difficult to find a measure of this, as its most radical exponents are reluctant to call themselves political scientists at all, even when they are teaching and writing about politics, and they are not very active in the affairs of the Political Studies Association. On the other hand, the behavioural school, which seeks to assimilate political science to natural science, is certainly stronger in the USA than it is here, and its exponents here sometimes talk as though they were isolated and unrecognized. But probably there is in fact a good deal of convergence. The American behaviourists have become more mature and sophisticated in their expectations: at the same time, main-stream political science in Britain (for instance, in electoral and local studies) has learnt a great deal from their techniques and from their discussions of methodology.

For various reasons, political science has been extremely lively and vigorous since 1945. This has been due partly to the growth of the social sciences in general, partly to the dramatic character of world politics during these years. But the debate owes much of its intellectual quality to this clash between main-stream political science and the 'ultras' on its flanks. The latter have forced us all to be more strict in definition and argument, and more sceptical about presuppositions, and there has been (we hope) a consequent rise in standards all round. Certainly, the triangular situation here described must be regarded as characteristic of the discipline at present, and as indispensable to it.

3. Topics in British political science

Classification

One effect of the debate in British political science is to raise questions about the proper way to classify work in progress: by problems, by techniques, by concepts, or by all three? It would be out of place to argue this here, and we have adopted a simple, and perhaps naïve, arrangement, designed primarily to emphasize problems of organization which concern the SSRC.

It should perhaps be stated explicitly that we should reject the idea that there is some sort of 'cut-off date', whether fixed or moving, which separates the past from the present, leaving the past to history and reserving the present for political science.

The classification is as follows:

Political Theory
>   The history of ideas
>   The analysis of political concepts
>   The 'great books'
>   The philosophy of the social sciences

British Government
>   Decision-making in general
>   Parliament
>   The Cabinet and the ministers
>   Central administration
>   Parties, voters, and elections
>   Interest groups
>   Élites
>   Local government and local politics

Regional government, and nationalism within the UK
Public corporations
Industrial relations

Comparative Politics
The political study of individual countries
The Empire and Commonwealth
Foreign institutions relevant to UK problems
Area studies

International Relations
The international political system
Foreign policy analysis
International institutions

Controversial innovations
General influences
Lines of research

Political Theory
As has been explained, it is characteristic of British political science that it has an open frontier on the side of the traditional humanities, and that no sharp line divides work on theory designed as the basis of research on current politics from work on the history of political ideas, on conceptual analysis, on the 'great books', and on political and social philosophy.

Work in political theory can be pursued by individuals with limited resources, it attracts able students, and it leads to work of high excellence. This in turn reinforces its attraction; and one can identify successive generations of scholars who have done distinguished work within this tradition. Perhaps four complementary aspects of it can be distinguished.

THE HISTORY OF IDEAS

At first, textbooks about the history of political thought were apt to isolate it from its context and to treat it as a series of episodes, in each of which some eminent thinker was the hero. This can still be justified as a teaching device, and the teacher can use material of this kind to formulate theory which he thinks apt to our contemporary situation.

But the trend now is towards a wider view of the history of ideas, a view which seeks to trace the links between political ideas and ideas about society, science, and religion, and to specify the character of this complex at chosen instants in the process of change. Work of this kind emphasizes continuity of tradition and the uniqueness of each historical situation. Many such authors would claim to be historians and philosophers, not social scientists, and some reject strongly the whole idea of social science as they understand it. Yet their contribution to the study of contemporary society is of great importance, in that they illustrate powerfully the idea that thought and language are interdependent with practice in all societies at all times.

THE ANALYSIS OF POLITICAL CONCEPTS

Another trend, to some extent parallel with the first, to some extent in opposition to it, is that which recommends scrupulous analysis of political words and concepts as used in political discourse by ordinary men and also by those who speak with authority in political life. 'Freedom', 'consent', 'justice', 'equality', 'rights', 'power', 'authority' will serve as examples. Philosophical analysis of terms was common before linguistic philosophy had arisen: the latter is important not as a new notion, but as a new twist to an old notion, inviting the analyst to analyze also his own process of analysis. Whatever colour we give it, this notion of a quest for precision through dialectics is very strong in traditional British training.

THE 'GREAT BOOKS'

To some extent, these two trends come together in the prescription of great books for study. But these are in general studied not as history, not as analysis, but as a sort of timeless dialogue about politics, involving the giants of political theory in the West. The canon of great books is variously defined, but it would include at least works by Plato, Aristotle, Augustine, Dante, Hobbes, Locke, Rousseau, Burke, J. S. Mill, and Marx; Montesquieu and de Tocqueville are strong claimants for admission. These books are perhaps instruments of teaching rather than subjects of research, in the most usual sense of the word 'research'; but they retain their vitality in the hands of teachers only if the work of editing and exposition is continually renewed. For instance, a 'mainstream' teacher of political science in this country would find that his exposition of *The Republic* has been substantially affected by Professor Ryle's recent book on Plato's political experience.[1]

At present substantial editorial work is being done on Hobbes, Locke, Adam Smith, Bentham, Burke, and Coleridge. This work is based on materials now available in the UK, but it is not well endowed, and faces strong American competition based on larger resources. There are rich collections of original material in Britain, and in general research workers and editors need only personal support while at work on it. But similar work in America is much better endowed, and there is always a risk that important research material may be lost to the UK. It is to be hoped that some

---

[1] Gilbert Ryle, *Plato's Progress* (Cambridge University Press, London, 1966).

financial help will be available to keep in the UK documents relevant to the history of political thought and of the social sciences in general.

The case is strongest where the documents relate to British writers. but it is also important that British workers in this field should look beyond British history to work in the larger world of European and American thought.

THE PHILOSOPHY OF THE SOCIAL SCIENCES

There have always been some British philosophers keenly interested in the practice and theory of politics and society, and 'Political Philosophy' or 'Social and Political Philosophy' still appears in the programmes of some universities. This is not as common as it was; indeed, political science has in some cases grown from philosophy departments and has become independent of them. Where the alliance survives (and some scholars at least feel strongly that it should be maintained), it means in practice that some aspects of theoretical teaching are in the hands of trained philosophers. Their tactics vary according to their own interests: but the general effect is to bring political theory closely into contact with philosophical controversies and trends, relating for instance to epistemology, to ethics, and to the nature of scientific and historical explanation.

It has been notable recently that where able philosophers tackle this problem they now feel obliged to discuss polity and society together, so that the field becomes 'political and social' or 'social and political' philosophy. It is also notable that the recent evolution of the social sciences has drawn the philosophers into discussion of methodology, and that in their hands methodological questions turn out also to be substantive questions about the nature of man and society. Professor Dorothy Emmet's two most recent books, *Functions, Purpose and Powers,* and *Rules, Roles and*

21

Relations[1] are individual examples of such thinking; there are other philosophers who have made important individual contributions.

There are two final observations to be made under the heading of 'political theory'.

First, there is a widespread feeling that political theory must not be segregated from the empirical study of politics. Some expressions of this feeling have been properly criticized as 'scientism'; nevertheless, there is great interest in the relation between political theory in the sense described hitherto and the general concepts used in descriptive and critical work about institutions. Some of the most difficult problems are those concerned with the relations between institutions, doctrines, and ideologies and their interaction with their intellectual and social setting; and there is growing interest in what is generally referred to as 'empirical political theory'. The phrase is not a very happy one, but it can be specified by reference to much of the work of Aristotle, Montesquieu, and de Tocqueville, as well as to the work of recent American theorists.

Secondly, there are some general considerations arising out of this section which are relevant to the next three sections.

So far as we can judge from reports of work in progress, most political scientists are oriented towards problems, not towards the development of theory or of technique. The ideal is still that a well-educated man, working alone or in a small group, should use such techniques as are available to him to document and analyze problems of central importance in British and world politics. Such work is 'academic' in the

---

[1] Dorothy Emmet, *Functions, Purpose and Powers* (Macmillan, London, 1958); *Rules, Roles and Relations* (Macmillan, London, 1966).

sense that it offers better analysis, more thorough documentation than can be expected from those who are engaged in practical politics; it should also be 'academic' in that it must be prepared to follow where the argument leads, even though the conclusion cuts across ordinary political alignments. But it is difficult to describe this procedure as 'scientific', since it lies open to criticism on two fronts. One wing of the opposition can claim fairly that most work of this kind, however cool in tone, is committed *a priori* to the notion of political improvement, of methodical self-help in politics, and that an open question of great philosophical importance is thus closed before work begins. The other wing can point out, with equal justification, that the work lacks rigour, both conceptually and in its technical procedure, and that practitioners make no attempt to establish a corpus of verified or verifiable theory as a basis for future progress.

These criticisms can to some extent be blunted by scrupulous care and patience in detail; but in the end the only effective answer is to turn them against the critics. Most practitioners of 'main-stream' political science in Britain would themselves see virtue in the opposition arguments, as necessary but impossible ideals. Their own problem is to find a philosophy with which to defend a middle position: to sustain the autonomy of academic work in politics, and yet to accept the burden of responsibility for acting politically as part of a living tradition of political freedom.

British Government

We do not distinguish here between 'politics' and 'public administration' because it is now a commonplace that the distinction breaks down at the highest levels of decision-making, in which politicians and administrators are involved together in a complex pattern of partnership and rivalry.

Indeed, it is not easy now to disentangle 'public' from 'private' administration, and it is tempting to define the political process as equivalent to the whole process of decision-making for the community, in so far as the formal procedures of the state are brought into play.

There is therefore an interesting field which involves the study of decision-making as such. This involves case studies of the origins of formal public decisions, great and small, and at the same time an attempt to conceptualize the decision-making process in a way which does justice to its real character, which is often disguised by constitutional forms and doctrines.

It is more difficult in Britain than in most democracies to document recent public decisions which are believed to be of political importance. This is one reason why it is important for political scientists to have access to material in the Public Record Office now that it has arrived there under the thirty-year rule. This will help to illuminate the recent past; as for contemporary decisions, it is true that the mild censorship which covers the origin of recent public decisions can be evaded or eroded (as in the book by Professor H. H. Wilson – an American – on the origins of commercial television),[1] but it will always be easier to study small public decisions than great ones, and this may be no less valuable as a means of exploring the political system.

A number of further topics in British government may be listed briefly.

The study of Parliament illustrates well how academic research is related to political currents. There is a long tradition of work on the procedure and history of Parliament, but this was rather slow to revive after World War II. At one time American work in the study of Congress was certainly

---

[1] H. H. Wilson, *Pressure Group. The Campaign for commercial television* (Secker and Warburg, London, 1961).

ahead of anything done in this country in the study of Parliament. But the situation changed during the 1950s, and there began a series of books about Parliament and its members, written with scholarly knowledge from various points of view. There is clearly an interesting relation (which might itself be the subject of research) between these books, the evidence presented by academics to Committees of the Commons, and the present public debate over the reform of Parliamentary procedure.

The Cabinet is of equal importance, but presents baffling difficulties to the scholar, greater (it seems) than does the study of the US Presidency. Much of what is written (and taught to students) about the relations between Prime Minister, Cabinet, Party, and Departments is based on traditional wisdom and on the interpretation of rather slender clues derived from personal sources. It is particularly important that scholars should take advantage of the thirty-year rule to establish a satisfactory model or models of how Cabinet government has worked in practice in relatively recent times.

The position is similar with regard to relations between the *central administration* and other public authorities, in particular public corporations and local authorities. For well-known constitutional reasons the work of the Civil Service has not been laid open to much academic scrutiny, and much of what is written is based on out-of-date experience and imperfect documentation. It is to be hoped that this situation will change as part of the modernization of the system itself; the recent RIPA study of central and local government (directed by Professor J. A. G. Griffith)[1] is a favourable omen.

---

[1] J. A. G. Griffith, *Central Departments and Local Authorities* (Allen and Unwin, London, 1966).

Work in this field is of course important also to economists, educationalists, and those concerned with social administration, who have all contributed a good deal to the little that is known about the character of our administrative system, its scope, and its limitations.

Parties, voters, and elections constitute together a field which presents fewer difficulties, and has been well tilled. But descriptive work is still needed to keep abreast of the continually changing practice of parties and elections, and little has been done to explore the self-selection and the social role of party activists at different levels of the system; or to study in depth the attitudes of voters and other participants and their change through time. Some useful work on this can be done by individual research based on case-studies: but on the whole these explorations of the sociology and psychology of the electoral system require fairly large combined operations, using surveys, panel studies, and data archives.

The relative weakness of British party organization in the 1950s diverted attention to two other topics of central importance, *interest groups* and *élites*.

Interest in 'group politics' was stimulated by recent American work, descriptive and conceptual, but it had its origin in the period of pluralist thought immediately before and after World War I. The theme, once rediscovered, slipped naturally into place in teaching and research, and is no longer an exciting novelty. But there is a need for continuing studies, provided that they are of high quality.

The study of *élites* became popular at the time when the 'Establishment' was a catch-word, and this also has taken its place easily in an older tradition. But concepts and documentation are still somewhat unsatisfactory, in spite of the work done by sociologists on social mobility, and some hard thinking is needed to clear the ground of prejudices and establish practicable research categories.

Local government is a field which has come alive in recent years, for various reasons. One reason why academic proposals for local-government reform have proved ineffective hitherto is that little is known and documented about the way in which local government actually works, politically and administratively. Once again, the Americans have been much ahead of us in the 'main-stream' job of analyzing and commenting on the political process at the local level. There has perhaps been more scientism or disguised philosophy in this American work than some scholars (both British and American) approve: but what has been done there shows that local government is a dull subject only where dull people study it, and that a great field of exploration is at the doorstep of every university in the country. A number of committees of inquiry (notably the Maud and Mallaby Committees on 'people in local government') have had finance provided by central government and by local authorities themselves for pioneer inquiries; and there is now a lively local government group within the PSA.

Regional government, and nationalism within the UK are also themes brought into prominence by current events. Hitherto there has been no real documentation either about centralization and its effects or about regional and national consciousness within the UK, and debate has simply drawn on a stock of unproven commonplaces. But in the last five years some currents in politics have been carrying events towards the development of regional institutions in England, and of national institutions in Wales and Scotland. At the same time, the experience of home rule in Northern Ireland presents problems very strange to the English. This complex of problems has theoretical as well as practical interest, and there is growing concern with it. From one point of view

27

the problem is an aspect of the 'crisis of national identity' through which the British are passing at present; from another point of view, it is concerned with the structure of administrative machinery and the deployment of administrators and professional experts. There has so far been little observation and analysis in this field, and it may prove to be of increasing importance.

Similarly, there are large gaps in our knowledge of the politics and administration of the *public corporations*. Something has been done (with Ministry of Health support) to begin empirical studies of hospital administration and the structure of the National Health Service; and the Nationalized Industries Committee of the House of Commons has let a little light into the problems of nationalized industries. But there has been far too little study in these administration fields, and this is essential if we are to discuss realistically the application of conclusions drawn from economic studies.

Finally, there is the field of *industrial relations*, which bridges politics, economics, and sociology. From one point of view, the government of industry is an aspect of contemporary politics, and it is important that studies of it should be based on realization of the issues of political theory and practice which are involved. It is thus important to bring political scientists into such studies : indeed, they can scarcely avoid being drawn in, as studies of parties, interest groups, and central administration are never complete without awareness of the industrial setting and its implications. Research in industrial relations is covered in a research review prepared by the Management and Industrial Relations Committee of the SSRC, which is being published separately.

Comparative Politics
British work on comparative politics has not till recently responded at all to the American dream of creating a general

science of political systems. But neither has it (on the whole) been guilty of the sins of 'arid institutionalism' of which the Americans used to accuse themselves. There are some older books, for instance on second chambers and on electoral systems, which are institutional in a rather abstract way: but most main-stream political scientists have been sternly educated in the historical tradition that each country must be studied as an individual case, and that no institution is intelligible except in its context. This has led perhaps to a certain parochialism in focus, but not to abstract presentation or wild generalization, which the Americans say are the sins of the older generation. Four strands can be separated.

THE POLITICAL STUDY OF INDIVIDUAL COUNTRIES

Brogan followed Bryce in the study of the political character of the USA, and both of them saw things not conspicuous to American scholars. The younger generation of British students of the USA are daunted by the sheer weight of American material and American talent; but British studies of France have been influential, in that they stand outside the French tradition and look across the Channel as if from another planet; and individual scholars have made conspicuous contributions to the study of other countries of Western and Eastern Europe.

THE EMPIRE AND COMMONWEALTH

This has created its own tradition of political study, which began with constitutional analysis of the Commonwealth in transition and of the diffusion within it of specific constitutional patterns, such as Cabinet government and federalism; and also with the study of colonial administration. British historians and political scientists followed these institutions through the transition to independence, and produced a body of work which has a high scholarly reputation. One immediate problem is to find means of building on this foundation now that we have lost our special facilities for access to a great political laboratory. This involves the maintenance of connections with colleagues and universities in the Commonwealth and ex-Commonwealth countries, and the provision of funds for research there. As was foreshadowed by the reports of the Hayter[1] and Parry[2] Committees, it also involves building new connections in Asian countries and in Latin America.

It seems inevitable that this extension of the range of comparison will increase the importance of theory. As the Americans have found, in taking the world as their province, the study of individual cases is not enough. One needs also tools of analysis for the study of political change in general, including study of the problems set by the widening gap between rich and poor nations. Comparative politics on this scale deals with issues which are of fundamental importance in international relations.

FOREIGN INSTITUTIONS RELEVANT TO UK PROBLEMS

There has been some but not much study of these: for instance, local government, the Ombudsman, parliamentary committees and public corporations in Sweden, French planning, the French École Nationale d'Administration. Such studies have been restricted by lack of funds and lack of official interest: in addition, academic doubt has clouded speculation about the transfer of institutions between systems. But in fact official enquiries have often been briefed hastily and badly about developments in other countries. Comparisons cannot be avoided; and if they are to be made it should be with adequate time and proper respect for

---

[1] *Report of the Sub-Committee on Oriental, Slavonic, East European and African Studies* (HMSO, London, 1961).

[2] University Grants Committee *Report of the Committee on Latin American Studies* (HMSO, London, 1965).

standards of scholarship. This requires a small but steady stream of research in progress, as a basis for *ad hoc* inquiry about topics that happen to become critical.

AREA STUDIES

The School of Slavonic and East European Studies and the School of Oriental and African Studies (London University) have long histories, and the recent expansion in area studies is in a sense a re-import of an old British and European idea which became fashionable in the USA in the 1950s. In the older British institutions the social sciences have now been drawn into association with linguistic and historical studies; a large number of area study centres have been founded as a result of the Scarbrough,[1] Hayter, and Parry reports; and some universities, old and new, have established such centres independently.

It is now accepted that the study of politics is an integral part of any regional study; and from this arise certain problems. Intellectually, there is a clash between the idea that understanding comes from the study of a complex of problems within an area that has cultural or geographical unity, and the idea that it comes from abstraction and comparison across the board. Is Middle Eastern politics (for instance) primarily part of the study of the Middle East, or primarily part of the study of politics? As a basis for inquiry, this can be a fruitful clash; but it is reflected in difficulties of organization and career structure. Few area study centres working on an interdisciplinary basis can have more than two or three political scientists as part of their team; and this is a small unit for political study. It therefore becomes important that they should also work closely with the political science

---

[1] Commonwealth Scholarship Commission, *First Annual Report, Second Annual Report* (Cmnd 1541, HMSO, London, 1961).

department in their university; and their career prospects will be improved if they take part in the general teaching of political science to undergraduates, so as to remain within the main stream of university development.

This dilemma is built into the nature of the situation and cannot be evaded. The right answer is certainly to encourage both interdisciplinary research within an area, and research within a discipline 'across the board'. But given limited resources of men and money, and the proliferation of area study centres in the UK, there will be difficult decisions about priorities.

International Relations

The Next Thirty Years Committee of the SSRC appointed two *ad hoc* panels of specialists to prepare reports on International Organization and on War Studies. These reports are published separately. The text of them was available when this section was prepared.

We have already noted that international relations developed in the universities closely linked with international history, and to a lesser extent with international law, at a time when political science was mainly concerned with the formal institutions of sovereign states, that is with the internal legal and constitutional nature of the *polis* rather than with diplomacy between states. Political science now construes its task more widely and in most cases includes some study of international relations; nevertheless, although the latter may not usually be regarded as a distinct discipline, it has a distinctive concern, namely, political activity at the level of diplomatic or international society, the relations between the members of that society, and the forces and factors, both internal and external, which affect these relations.

Moreover, the subject retains its close links with international history. Thus, on the one hand, in the tradition of political science (or, perhaps more accurately, of political sociology) the study of international relations attempts to discover in the welter of diplomatic events that which is characteristic, typical; its method is usually comparative and its concern is to arrive at valid propositions about the nature of political activity at the international level. On the other hand, international history, either as part of or closely allied to international relations, provides the raw material for the formulation and testing of these propositions; it gives depth and perspective to the study of the present; and above all it can impart the sense of the concrete, of the particular and the contingent in human affairs, which is an enriching experience in itself and a check upon over-ready generalization.

Two further comments may be in order. The first is that, in general, contemporary academic studies of international relations have parted company with the rather policy-oriented and idealistic preconceptions of the inter-war period (at least of the 1920s). Concern with what *is* has generally replaced anxiety about what *ought* to be. This is not an either/or distinction; but the emphasis has certainly shifted. The second is that it is difficult, if not impossible, to disentangle many problems of international relations from those of the human situation as a whole. There are problems of world economics, there are social problems, such as those of race, class, and nation, and there are problems within the realm of the natural sciences, such as those ol food production, birth control, etc., all of which have a bearing on international relations. Consequently, international relations specialists are well aware of the contribution of other disciplines to their own studies; indeed, the essentially interdisciplinary nature of a good deal of the research in international relations is generally welcomed as, amongst other things, a healthy corrective to over-specialization.

The manner in which the subject has developed reflects,

of course, the particular circumstances of the universities where it is to be found. As is to be expected in a rapidly growing subject in which there is lively discussion over problems of scope and methodology, there is considerable diversity of opinion as to what are the chief growing-points or, indeed, what is the main stem. Nevertheless, there are three main aspects of international relations which usually figure in universities, though the nomenclature and style may differ greatly from one to another. The first, the *international political system*, covers the emergence and growth of the system of sovereign states (from the sixteenth century to the present), and the political processes at work within it. The second, *foreign policy analysis*, is concerned with how foreign policy is made and executed. The third, *international institutions*, involves the identification and examination of the well-established rules and usages of international society, and the assessment of their contribution, whether they are world-wide or regional, to the maintenance and strengthening of world order. Each of these will now be looked at in rather more detail.

THE INTERNATIONAL POLITICAL SYSTEM

The concern here is with the environment in which states act; the focus may be on the origins and development of the system over the last 400 years or so, examining for instance its changing structure, the shifting power configurations, the sources of conflict and conflagration, the elements of stability and change. Or comparative analyses may be attempted of the different types of system over the last few centuries, attempting to discern the special characteristics of each and the manner in which one gave place to another. There might also be included here studies of the causes and nature of international armed conflict. The aim here is rather to increase the understanding of the nature of war as a contingency of the international system than to devise specific techniques for preventing or waging it. This would also include the field of crisis management, whether the study of crises is analytically handled through the techniques of games theory and simulation, or based in a more traditional manner on historical case studies. It might also cover peace studies, defined as the avoidance, elimination, and control of force; for example the constraints upon the use of force, and, in general, the study of the bases and instruments of international order: balance of power, economic inter-dependence, international law and morality, and systems of alliance.

FOREIGN POLICY ANALYSIS

This is concerned with how foreign policy is made and exe-cuted in individual states. That is to say, it inquires how the political sub-systems, or states, which compose the inter-national system, see and are affected by their environment. From one point of view this is an aspect of the political pro-cess in each individual state, and so is bound up with a study of the state's political system as a whole. But the process of reaction and adaptation to the external situation can to some extent be extracted for purposes of comparison, if only be-cause it takes place within an environment common to all states. There are, therefore, possibilities of fruitful compari-son of different types of reaction to similar situations. There is also the possibility of less abstract comparison of the manners in which foreign policies are formulated (for in-stance, through study of the role of interest groups, constitu-tional machinery, etc.) as well as of the means by which policy is implemented (for instance, the methods of pressure and of influence as well as the instrumentalities). Here defence studies would normally also be included – the defence capa-bilities and commitments of states, the place of the armed forces within the state, and more specialist issues such as defence policy-making, the techniques of defence management, weapons procurement and the like. The implications of rapidly changing weapon technology might also be expected to figure here, as also in the study of the international political system.

INTERNATIONAL INSTITUTIONS

This is another large field of study. There is, first, the detailed study of the traditional institutions of world order: the systems of the balance of power, and of international law and diplomacy; and the pattern of alliances and regional systems.

Second, there is the history and practice of international institutions of a general character, such as the League of Nations and the United Nations. On the political side this would include the study of techniques of conciliation and mediation and of pacific settlement generally, of the problems of disarmament and arms control, and in recent years of the role of international institutions in the containment of conflict and in the process of decolonization.

Then, on the economic side, there is the relationship between world economic institutions and the international economic system, as well as the role of private economic organizations in that system, and the problems, for instance, of international economic aid and of economic co-operation between industrialized countries. This might in some instances extend into an examination of the 'functional' specialized agencies concerned primarily with economic and social problems, such as the Food and Agricultural Organization or the International Labour Organization.

The growth of regional institutions, economic and political, has been of increasing interest in recent years. The political as well as the economic and legal aspects of the European communities have attracted particular attention, but interest extends to similar attempts at politico-economic integration in Scandinavia, Eastern Europe, Africa, and Central and Latin America.

Finally, there is the study of the structure of international institutions in terms both of the problem of co-ordinating and evaluating their operations and of the growth of an international civil service in many ways distinct from the traditional diplomatic services of member states.

To these main features of the subject may be added more specialist studies of twentieth-century political ideas and movements, in terms both of theory and practice: strategic studies, dealing with the role of force in international relations, the techniques of managing the use of force, and of such more recent issues as those of deterrence, limited conflict, and policing techniques; the politics of international economic relations, looking at the sources and organization of national economic power in relation to foreign policy, and the political aspects of some major international economic issues; and the sociology of international law, which examines the function and role of international law both in relation to the international system and as a restraint upon, and instrument of, national foreign policy. Students are also concerned with historical case-studies in which the functioning of the international political system and the behaviour of its members can be seen in microcosm, for example, the balance of power viewed historically, or the Suez Crisis, or the Paris Peace Conference of 1919, or an aspect of twentieth-century Anglo-American relations, or the Manchurian Crisis of 1931–3.

In even such an inevitably brief and patchy account as this, some mention should be made of the controversy about attempts to build a general theory of international relations. The absence of any such general theory continues to disturb some, while others – regarding this in much the same light as the human condition – are sceptical, wondering if any single theoretical system is not as likely to mislead and distort as to enlighten. Some argue that the academic theorist's job is to elicit and criticize the presuppositions of thought about the nature of international society and the relations between its members by maintaining and developing the classical tradition of political theory in the West. They are concerned with the growth of international thought as expressed in the political, legal, and historical writing of such writers as Machiavelli, Hobbes, Grotius, Ranke, etc., and with the problems of international theory dealing with, for instance, the consequences of anarchy in international relations, the working of the system of the balance of power, the problem of the 'just' war, the question of the right of intervention, etc.

Others, though still very much a minority, prefer to draw on the most recent developments in the study of physical and biological systems, using models drawn from the formulations (mathematical or other) of general systems theory, information theory, games theory, the theory of networks, and so on. They look to the formulation of general theory, using precisely defined terms, by which they hope to produce testable propositions; that is to say, they regard the study of the international system as being a science, like other sciences, beset with difficulties, but capable of improvement. Some of those in this behaviouralist vein may be more sceptical about the possibilities of evolving a general theory and may be more concerned to evolve partial theories in, for instance, the realm of systems analysis, which may help evolve a typology of differing international systems; or of communication analysis, which may indicate the processes of international integration or community building; or of conflict research, which may identify the sources, and even perhaps assist the resolution of, international conflicts.

As in other sectors of political studies, this clash of views about the role of theory has made this period an intellectually exciting one. There is some risk that differences in theoretical style may lead to mutual incomprehensibility, and so to rigid maintenance of fixed positions. Yet both those in the classical tradition and the contemporary behaviouralists share an interest in specific theoretical questions. The end of it may be that all schools will be drawn together – the lion with the lamb, the hawk with the dove; but that is not the present position, and the most immediate need is to prevent a breakdown in the dialogue about theory.

It should be added that there is a sense in which all students of international relations (including the theorists) claim history as their own. The pragmatists appeal to it as the source of tradition and of evidence about traditional behaviour; the model-builders are concerned to analyse historical trends and crises in formal terms, as this is as yet the only reliable and readily available laboratory in which to test their models. Adequate documentation, even for case-study work in contemporary history, is not always as difficult as is sometimes made out, but many of the studies outlined above are dependent to an important extent on the early release of documents by governments – and of ready access to them. A consequence of this is that all students of international relations are concerned with problems of archives and their availability.

Controversial innovations

The existence of two wings of opinion critical of 'mainstream' political science has already been mentioned (p 15). Both wings are important, but only one needs substantial discussion here: that associated with the behavioural movement in the USA.

European philosophies and sociologies of politics, in

particular those of Marx and Weber, there met a strong local tradition of empirical study directed to immediate social gains. The amalgam has a flavour of its own, conspicuously 'un-English' but fascinating to English students in its own right and as an expression of one aspect of the American political scene. The demand for the 'behavioural study of politics' had the character of a crusade in the USA in the 1950s, and provoked violent controversy within the American Political Science Association. The controversy has now grown milder and more sophisticated, and 'behaviouralism' in some form is accepted as one component of the discipline in virtually all American universities. But meanwhile the controversy has been exported, and has stimulated discussion in all countries where political science is taught.

Behind the doctrine or fashion lies the great American tradition that there is no problem that men cannot solve if they deploy enough energy and enough brains with enough persistence. If technological problems can be solved like that, why not political ones? What is government but another technology?

In a sense, these questions can be answered out of the 'great books', or at least the pattern of argument about them can be foreseen. The sceptics and the enthusiasts are in opposition about the nature of man and society; the main stream think cautiously in terms of the incidental gains and losses from a dispute which cannot be finally resolved. There is a strong case for thinking that at present the gains outweigh the losses, and that much can be learnt, though the final goal cannot be attained.

GENERAL INFLUENCES

There are at least three grounds for this belief.

First, there is the progress of social science in general. There is now much systematic knowledge about the operation of human groups and of individuals within them; it is not wholly new, in that much was foreshadowed by the insight of philosophers, historians, poets, and novelists, but these insights have now been formalized and demonstrated in a tolerably rigorous way. The gains made by social psychology, social anthropology, and the sociology of small groups are modest but genuine, and there is no reason to doubt that more can be gained by further exploration. Studies at this level include studies of politics on a small scale. There is debate about the proper use of the word 'politics' in this context, and also about the nature of the gap (which all recognize) between the politics of small groups and of tribal societies and the politics of states. But certainly the study of micro-politics makes progress, and political scientists cannot disregard it, though their primary concern is with macro-politics, the politics of states and of the system of states.

At that level the situation is rather different. During the past century political theory and sociological theory have converged, so that they are quite frequently taught as a single subject, at least at the more advanced levels. They share a dispute about the possibility and value of 'over-arching theory' or 'grand theory': the dispute is inconclusive but complex and lively, and there have been signs recently that economists perplexed over the summation of individual preferences are ready to make their own contribution to theoretical debate at that level.

Undoubtedly the economists have made more progress than anyone else in empirical study of the macrocosm, and a vast amount is known about world economy and the economics of individual states. But it is increasingly realized that economic knowledge cannot be used for public purposes except through politics; this was perhaps grasped first as a result of experience in developing countries, but there would be agreement now that the proposition is a general one.

Hence it is generally realized that we cannot use economics better till we understand politics better; and political science is thus drawn almost irresistibly to make plans for attack on empirical problems of extreme difficulty and importance; problems which concern the mechanism of human foresight and planning in human affairs, and the limits set to its effectiveness by the character of human society.

Secondly, there has been much recent exploration of problems of methodology in the natural sciences and in social science. 'The science of science' is still in its earliest stages; but it has already indicated to political scientists that the making of policy about science is a key point in all advanced states, and also that no one need be much alarmed about the problem of 'the two cultures'. The old notion that there is something which is *the* scientific method is breaking up into various elements, and there is no longer any need to postulate that *either* social science is like physics *or* it is unscientific.

This discussion has emphasized the power and the limitations of formalized reasoning and of models based on it. At the same time there have appeared bodies of propositions which are in fact quite 'pure' mathematically, but which reflect social rather than physical interests. This appears for instance from such names as games theory, information theory, decision theory, and cybernetics. These, taken with statistical theory in general, offer tools for handling very large numbers of interdependent variables related to one another in a 'system'; hence attempts (Easton,[1] Kaplan[2]) to formalize the political system (national or international) within a framework of 'general systems theory'.

---

[1] David Easton, *A Systems Analysis of Political Life* (Wiley, N.Y., 1965).

[2] Morton A. Kaplan, *System and Process in International Politics* (Wiley, N.Y., 1957; Chapman and Hall, London, 1958).

There is no doubt about the elegance of these models, and of their power as analogies indicating points of inquiry. It is, however, still doubtful whether we can find 'political quantities' (even in the shape of weak orderings) to use in the models, and without measurement we cannot hope to make much progress in explanation and prediction by these methods.

Thirdly, there has at the same time been an 'explosion' in the amount of information available and in techniques for processing it. A glance at Russett's *World Handbook of Political Indicators*[1] (or at the material in Banks and Textor's *Cross-Polity Survey*[2]), will indicate what has been done and what might be done. Very large quantities of data are available for each country in the world, and it is possible to make some guess at their margins of error (which are in some cases high). These data, with indications of their limits, can be fed into a computer, and correlations can be established. Many of these indicate results which seem to be right, judged by common sense, and it is something to be able to reinforce the findings of common sense. Not much more than this is claimed by sophisticated operators at present; but it is enough to encourage them to go further.

LINES OF RESEARCH
These three influences (the growth of social science, new methods of formalization, and the 'data revolution') reinforce one another, and give quite substantial grounds for investment in new lines of political research. The cost involved

---

[1] B. M. Russett *et al., World Handbook of Political and Social Indicators* (Yale University Press, 1964).
[2] A. S. Banks and R. Textor, *A Cross-Polity Survey* (MIT Press, Mass., 1963).

is not large, by American standards, and it would be justified even by modest gains in understanding.

First, there are behavioural studies in various forms. Obvious branches are electoral behaviour, legislative behaviour 'Eulau[1] and others), judicial behaviour (Glendon Schubert[2] and others); indeed, the method can be tried in any field in which numbers such as voting statistics or judicial statistics are readily available. The first wave of such studies was strong on correlations, rather weak in explanation; in other words, it was not at all good at producing general theory, and scarcely made an attempt at testable propositions based on general theory.

The Americans have been well aware of this, and later studies (for instance, Almond and Verba, *The Civic Culture*)[3] have been tied fairly strictly to general theories of social psychology, using in particular such concepts as culture, socialization, level of aspiration, and salience. The theory is not in a very satisfactory state even yet; in particular, there is no clearly agreed view about the conceptual relation between 'political culture' and 'political system', and it is sometimes difficult to be certain whether differences of view between different scholars are substantial, or simply the result of poor standardization of terminology. Electoral studies and public opinion studies in Britain have on the whole skirted the fringes of this theoretical morass, and have produced limited but influential results. The large American studies have been very impressive technically, and have had an even greater effect on the campaigning tactics of politicians than

---

[1] Heinz Eulau & J. C. Wahlke, *Legislative Behavior: A Reader in Theory and Practice*, (Glencoe, 1959).

[2] Glendon Schubert, *Quantitative Analysis of Judicial Behaviour* (Glencoe, 1959).

[3] Gabriel Almond and S. Verba, *The Civic Culture: political attitudes and democracy in five nations* (Princeton University Press, 1963).

have the British studies. Nuffield College is jointly engaged
with the Survey Research Center at the University of Michi-
gan on a study of British political attitudes, involving three
waves of interviews made before and after the elections of
1964 and 1966. Future plans must to some extent depend on
the outcome of this major study.

These studies have generally been psychological in style,
and based primarily on survey research. It is possible to distinguish (secondly) a parallel but independent stream of
'ecological' research, using primarily the concepts of structural sociology and of human geography, and the data which
are available in many government archives in Western
Europe for voting figures at the local level. Such figures can
be set alongside figures for party membership, education, income, employment, religion, mobility and so on; and one can
build an archive for the correlation of changes in these factors through time. There is thus a tool for the analysis of
social structure, social change, and their relation to politics;
and the results may be valuable as history even if they offer
no guide to present and future trends.

This sort of political arithmetic is associated in the first
instance with André Siegfried in France and Herbert Tingsten[1] in Sweden. It depends on the availability of good series
of official statistics for small all-purpose units of administration which remain the same over long periods; hence perhaps
its early start in France and Scandinavia, where it is still very
strong.

The British and American adminstrative systems have not
produced statistical series of this kind, and great labour will
be needed to piece these together. The Americans have be-

---

[1] Herbert Tingsten, *Political Behaviour: Studies in Election
Statistics*, tr. V. Hammarling, Stockholm Economic Studies No. 7
(P. S. King & Son, London, 1937).

gun to create data archives covering all elections, federal and state, since 1789; and a pilot study is in progress for a national data centre in Washington. While he was at Yale, Professor Karl Deutsch launched the idea of a world archive of data relevant to comparative politics, of which the *World Handbook* referred to above is the first-fruit. In Britain considerable interest in this approach has been shown by social and economic historians and geographers as well as by political scientists; but a great deal of work is needed to produce even limited series of comparable data.

In this section, we should perhaps include the work of the late L. F. Richardson,[1] himself a biologist, on the statistics of deadly conflicts and of arms races. His pioneering work was in itself inconclusive, but it has indicated important lines of inquiry into the character of world politics as a biological system operating within a changing natural environment.

Thirdly, there has been an attack, more limited in scope, on the problems of political language. It is an old story that politics (even violent politics) is largely a matter of words, and that skill in using and interpreting verbal communication is perhaps the supreme political skill; in fact, that rhetoric is the key to politics. The older writers are full of perceptive commonplaces and illuminating anecdotes on this topic; but in the past the labour of close analysis has been largely left to grammarians and classical scholars. Content analysis as a tool of political inquiry first became important during World War II, when it was used to search enemy propaganda for clues as to enemy intentions; and after the war Professor Lasswell and his followers were for a time interested in content analysis as a means of measurement in the study of political symbols. The technique then went somewhat out of fashion, perhaps because Lasswell's interests changed, per-

---

[1] L. F. Richardson, *Statistics of Deadly Quarrels* (Stevens. London, 1960).

haps because organized content analysis by a team did not show sufficient gains compared with sampling by a single skilful and experienced reader. But in recent years there has been a revival, due partly to the invention of devices for typing a text straight into a computer, so that much more analysis can be carried out and the importance of the human element is reduced. (This is of course related to the problems of machine translation, on which much money has been spent.)

There has also been growing interest in the study of language and other means of communication within small groups, and Bernstein's[1] work on socio-linguistics has considerable importance for anyone concerned with the character of political argument. This perhaps belongs to a *fourth* category of inquiry, that of laboratory research into leadership, co-operation, and conflict in small groups, generally by some sort of simulation. Such experiments are clearly in some sense relevant to politics, and in America some political scientists have co-operated profitably in laboratory research. But analysis of earlier work of this kind indicates that great skill and caution is needed to specify the conditions of an experiment and to ensure that no unknown factors are present and unnoticed. It is true that such procedures shade off by stages from laboratory research under rigorous conditions to simulation of a very general kind used primarily as a teaching device, and that some profitable use can be found for the device in each of its forms. But it is extremely important, and not easy, to define each form rigorously, and not to extend a conclusion beyond its defined setting without further experiment.

One of the live questions in political theory at the moment

---

[1] Basil Bernstein, 'A Socio-linguistic Approach to Social Learning,' *Penguin Survey of the Social Sciences*, ed. Julius Gould (Penguin, Harmondsworth, 1965).

is whether the 'cybernetic model' of a political system as being adaptive within an environment is worth anything except as an analogy. The model is undoubtedly a powerful tool in the natural sciences, particularly in biology and ecology; but political theory has fed on analogies since its origin, and it would be natural that it should adopt a new scientific analogy from new scientific language. It is claimed, however, that this is more than an analogy, that it is not on the same footing as Hobbes's analogy between a polity and a man, or Burke's analogy with a tree.

The key point of the theory is that system maintenance requires not only mass/energy but also information, and it invokes the modern mathematics of information theory. This has great attractions as a heuristic model in politics: political activity is certainly in some sense determined by political information. But it is in fact extremely difficult to measure (even crudely) the information which passes in a political system in real life; and it is not easy to see how progress can be made except by analysis under artificial conditions.

On the whole, attempts to use as laboratory some bounded area of a larger system have not worked well. There was a phase in the 1950s when American political scientists sought to use local communities as laboratories for the study of political power in America: but the results were ambiguous, for reasons now clear after a very lively *post mortem*. This does not destroy the idea that the study of local communities is relevant to the study of national politics; the study remains important, but as a substantive branch of study, and not merely as a laboratory for the testing of general concepts. Clearly, rigorous testing is not possible within local communities as open and as diverse as those of Western states. We can perhaps depend to some extent on theoretical models drawn from the observation of isolated tribal communities, but we shall find it very difficult to use any part of the life of a Western state as a laboratory in isolation from the political system as a whole. Hence, there is a continuing interest among political scientists in the possibility of rigorous conceptualization and experiment in artificial situations, though we are ill-equipped to carry out the work ourselves.

4. Objects to be achieved

Logically this chapter should perhaps have come earlier; objects to be achieved usually precede projects. We have not felt this logical scheme to be binding on us because our approach has been to discover, first, what political scientists are doing and are anxious to do, then to assess what they propose in relation to the resources available. The objects of our studies are diverse but can be summarized quite briefly.

There are a few who believe that we can at some date, however remote, achieve a political science sufficiently comprehensive to be a general guide to action. There would be general agreement that this is an illusion, since each political decision is an individual case, and cannot be dominated by general laws of a statistical character. A few regard the illusions of scientism as dangerous; most regard them as a necessary ingredient in the political process and in political inquiry.

There would perhaps be more general agreement with the opposite view, that political study, like historical study, should be engaged in for its own sake, not to elicit laws or to benefit mankind. In this sense, political science is one of the 'humanities', though one concerned with the present as well as with the past. The object of this sort of political science is to understand politics, and this (it would be said) is in itself sufficient. Understanding is necessary to successful action, but it will be clouded if extraneous purposes are introduced prematurely. In this sense, the discipline is to be regarded as a purpose in itself.

The main body of political scientists would, however, claim more; that the state of political science in a country or a period is in itself an indicator of political character, and that political science serves a country (and the world) as part of the information system which makes adaptation possible in time. The former point is easy to illustrate throughout history and in the contemporary world. The trends of political science in Western universities, particularly in the USA, the UK, France, and Scandinavia, have been closely related to the trends of politics in these countries; not as a source of power in politics, but as a special sort of reflection about politics. From this point of view it is interesting to watch the development of political teaching and inquiry in countries which are in a state of political transition and uncertainty: for instance, in Poland, West Germany, India, and Japan.

The latter point depends on the cybernetic analogy, or on Bertrand de Jouvenel's metaphor of the look-out tower, *la vigie*. The minimum requirements of a working political system is that it achieves self-preservation by short-term adaptations to environment. Political science (with other social sciences) would claim for itself more than this; that the study of politics makes it possible to think of a rather longer horizon and of a second level: not only reaction to circumstances, but the adaptation of the institutions on which the response depends. It would claim also that it quickens adaptation by helping to develop a body of politically literate citizens, sharing a set of perspectives even though they disagree about action.

It is not perhaps generally realized that the political scientists in the universities are part of a very widely based system of politics teaching in the country. On the one hand, publicists writing and talking for mass media are greatly influenced by serious research work in the universities, and transmit it (not uncritically) to wider audiences, which include many practising politicians and administrators. On the other hand, many good students go into the non-university sector of higher education, to teach for examinations outside the universities or to experiment with liberal studies in technical colleges. Many of them do devoted work with quite inadequate facilities: but it is uncertain what effect their teaching has in broadening the circle of political education. There seems to be no doubt that they have to some extent cut into the traditional realm of extra-mural adult education, but the latter has traditionally been associated with politics teaching and it still shows much vitality in that field. So far, the impact of the social sciences on the teacher-training colleges has not been large, and political science has been excluded altogether, except from the colleges training teachers for further education. There has in consequence been little thought about the process of 'political socialization' of young people, and very little is known about how British children learn an 'operative code' of politics (not merely party allegiance), what that code is, and how strongly it is held. The political role of teaching about politics might itself be an important topic for long-term research.

Next comes the question of the direct participation of political scientists in attempts at political improvement, and whether their recommendations are useful.

At the level of organization and methods in public administration, the British contribution has hitherto been negligible; there has been so far very limited interchange between work in the universities and work in public authorities, a matter of faults on both sides. But the RIPA has done much useful work of this kind, and it is to be hoped that the Institutes of Local Government at Birmingham and Strathclyde can establish good working relations with local authorities, once the latter have passed through the present phase of anxiety about structural reform. Similarly, it is to be hoped that the RIPA and the universities will be closely associated with further developments of Civil Service training and research. Hitherto there has been a vicious circle, comparable to that in management training and research: the universities have not had much to offer in the way of operational training (as distinct from liberal studies) because they have had neither funds nor access for operational research. The situation has begun to change in the field of social administration, but public administration still lags.

Work at this 'O and M' level is not to be sharply distinguished from work concerned with political institutions. People in government, like people in business, often fail to realize how they are spending their time; often an objective record of what they in fact do diverges so much from what they think they do that the case for change becomes unassailable. Much recent research into the operation of the House of Commons and of local authorities has been of this character. But more often suggestions for political improvement involve an appeal to standards which are themselves disputable; for instance, about the balance between Cabinet and Commons, or between front-benchers and back-benchers in the Commons. Political scientists should be trained to grasp quickly the history and law of a given institution, to observe its practice scrupulously, and to apply standards only with an explicit statement of their origin and justification. It is an article of faith that if these rules are observed then the political scientist's analysis will help the discussion forward. The faith itself implies an optimistic view of politics, but on the whole it is the professional creed of the discipline. Quite a number of political scientists have become MPs recently, and perhaps their knowledge and contacts helped them in their careers. But the discipline itself is oriented not to the training of politicians but to objective analysis of the polity. This is why political theory of a traditional kind is so important to it.

At the level of comparative politics and international

politics it is idle to hope that political science can promote much improvement directly. At most, it can maintain international connections that make a tiny contribution to the adaptability of the international system; and it can help to make the British, at all levels, a little more sensitive to the character of international politics and to its fluctuations.

Indeed, political science is in a sense an export trade, in that international reputation depends to a certain extent on the export of ideas and of books. We have just come to the end of a period of some two hundred years during which British institutions were highly regarded as a model, and one line of study in comparative politics is to pursue these institutions through different settings, and to analyse the process of transmission and adaptation. It would be hard to show that this process of export did good or harm to the British themselves; but certainly it was a mark of international prestige, and certainly the 'great books' of British constitutional history, constitutional law, and political analysis played an essential part in transmission. Similarly, it is hard to show that British studies of international law and politics have improved the conduct of British foreign policy: but they have certainly marked Britain's position as a centre of thought and influence in world affairs. It is unlikely that Britain reduced to the status of off-shore island will be as influential in shaping world politics as in the days of imperial greatness. But the saying that Minerva's owl flies only in the twilight may be relevant; it may be possible to achieve greater intellectual insight and independence now than during the imperial period, and to sustain an important part in the continuing debate about world politics.

5. Resources required

Certain conclusions flow directly from this analysis of human resources, research interests, and research objectives. These are set out here under three headings, which overlap somewhat: help to individuals, general facilities, and research overseas.

Help to individuals
The inquiry directed to members of the Political Studies Association brought out clearly how much depends on the contribution of individual university teachers. There are in the country some forty departments of political science and international relations, and many of them are quite small. Even a modest teaching programme in politics covers a wide range of topics, and the flow of publication perhaps affects political science more than it does any other social science, as the daily stream of news and public pronouncements must be digested, as well as academic books and articles. It is easy to say that there are too many small departments: but in fact this flows from the decision to have many medium-sized universities rather than a few very large ones. It is hard to imagine a Western university which does not include the teaching of politics in some form (not necessarily under that name), and the cost of achieving this has been that some of the departments in old and new universities are very small. It is not altogether easy to define 'department' in a way free from ambiguity: in very general terms we might say that half of the departments about which we have information have fewer than ten members, including the head of the department, and that two-thirds of the political scientists

teaching in universities are in departments with less than fifteen members.

We have no similar data for departments teaching to degree standard in the non-university sector of higher education, but information gained in other ways indicates that the position there is in all respects worse, and that it is common to find departments with two or three teachers (and negligible library resources) teaching for the finals of the B.Sc. (Econ.), the Diploma in Municipal Administration, and other external examinations of degree standard. There is little chance of any substantial change in this situation during the next five years, even on the most optimistic view.

It might be argued that support for research should be concentrated in places where the University Grants Committee and the universities have decided to back strong departments. It is inevitable that this should happen to some extent, because stronger departments are likely to attract better staff, to use them more effectively, and to submit better projects. But it is important for the health of the subject that small departments and those who teach in them should be given an opportunity to contribute to research.

These needs of individual research workers may be summarized as follows.

ACCESS TO LIBRARIES

The UGC Report on Libraries (the Parry Report)[1] gives an idea of the general position and attempts to suggest standards of expenditure. Some institutions do not meet their responsibilities to their staff and students in this respect: but clearly the flood of publication is now so great that the smaller institutions cannot hope to possess adequate research libraries

---

[1] University Grants Committee, *Report of the Committee on Libraries* (HMSO, London, 1967).

except in very narrow fields. Hence the need for co-operation regionally and nationally; the lines of thought of the Parry Report are (briefly) these:

(a) Co-operative purchasing arrangements, such as are beginning to develop among the Institutes of African Studies and Latin-American Studies.

(b) Development of a National Library for periodicals in the social sciences: the National Lending Library for Science and Technology at Boston Spa has now taken over this responsibility. It can produce a copy or photo-copy of an article very quickly, at a small cost to the university sponsoring a request.

(c) Development of a National Lending Library for books in the social sciences; the Parry Report strongly recommends this, but the matter is still undecided pending settlement of responsibilities between the British Museum, the National Lending Library, and the present National Central Library.

(d) Attention to the national collections of newspapers and other periodicals, British and foreign.

TIME FOR RESEARCH

Perhaps some universities are not as generous as they should be in granting sabbatical leave, paid or unpaid; but there are real difficulties which arise from teaching commitments in small departments and from the family obligations of young married people. The SSRC research fellowships as they exist at present are not designed to meet the needs of serving members of university staff seeking to continue and complete research in progress or to initiate new projects. It is of course open to them to apply for a research grant including salary during leave of absence. but it might be simpler and more convenient to handle such cases through an extension of the Fellowship scheme.

ROUTINE ASSISTANCE

Perhaps the position is improving slowly, but in general universities have paid little attention to recommendations that they should economize the time of specialists by providing adequate ancillary staff. Indeed, no attempt has been made to establish reasonable standards of overhead expenditure for backing social science departments, as has been done quite generously in the natural sciences and in engineering.

TRAVEL

Universities vary also in their readiness to finance travel in Britain for research and for research conferences, and few provide any funds at all for travel outside Britain.

These difficulties arise partly from the nature of small departments, partly because universities do not appreciate that in the social sciences as in the natural sciences, productivity in teaching and research depends to some extent on adequate capitalization.

FREEDOM OF SCOPE

In some kinds of political research it is almost impossible to draw a line between the social sciences and the humanities. It would, for instance, be impossible to say that the study of Aristotle's political and rhetorical works is not political science, or to exclude editorial work on (for instance) Marx or Pareto. Much has been written about differences in attitude between research workers in the social sciences and in the humanities, but the distinction is hard to draw in political science, which is concerned with the relevance of all human experience to a particular set of problems. Indeed, it may positively hamper and distort new lines of work if there is too much insistence on boundaries between disciplines, faculties, and grant-giving authorities.

58

General facilities

The Political Science Committee has had referred to it a number of matters concerning services of value to the social sciences in general, though political science is the major user. Action is in progress on four such matters, each extremely complex and important, and we have added two others.

SURVEY DATA ARCHIVE

This has been approved in principle, and action is now at a critical stage. It may be several years before we can see how successful the experiment has been, but it has great promise as an instrument for co-ordinating and exploiting research data. Our major interest must be for some time in developing the Essex Centre and in linking to it other suppliers and users of data; but this need not exclude the development of smaller local centres for data storage and processing.

ECOLOGICAL ARCHIVE

The relevance of this, and its difficulties, are indicated on p. 45 above. It is a commonplace that the statistics generated by British administration (especially local administration) are extremely difficult to use for statistical research. They are collected on different bases for different areas and for different periods, and it is very difficult to establish adequate series topic by topic, as the figures for different topics interlock. At present, one may sometimes get more reliable results more quickly by sample survey than by attempting to re-analyze official figures: a sample of 1,000 interviews does not cost much more than to hire a specialist assistant for a year. But it is not (surely) beyond the wit of man to improve this situation, and at least to make as much progress as has been made since the 1930s in statistics related to economic policy. It is not clear where the responsibility lies for securing these improvements: it is more than can be handled by the

59

Registrar General's Office as at present constituted, and it may in the end need a separate organization as strong as the Central Statistical Office. It may, however, be necessary for the SSRC to take the initiative in trying to make a long-term plan for the collection and processing of political and social data which arise from the business of administrative authorities, or are collected by them. In a sense, this is a problem of public administration and thus of special concern to our committee; but it involves all the social sciences and the medical sciences as well, and it will be a long job to get data-collection and data-processing into a form which facilitates social research and social control. The special requirements of political research are of great interest to us, but are perhaps secondary.

PRESS-CUTTING SERVICES

The problems of collecting and storing British and foreign newspapers were referred to on p. 57. These involve national library organization, and it is meantime a matter of urgency that we should not lose the most valuable instrument we have, that of press-cutting services focused in various ways. The library of cuttings maintained at Chatham House is quite essential to students of international affairs and merits support.

RECENT ARCHIVES AT THE PUBLIC RECORD OFFICE

Students of twentieth-century archives experience difficulties because of pressure on the space and resources of the PRO. These difficulties have been increased now that the archives are opened after thirty years; material of this kind is vital for research into administrative institutions, and for some topics even a thirty-year rule imposes undue restrictions on the process of learning by the analysis of experience. But the sheer bulk of the records is intimidating, and it may be that the problem cannot be solved within the limits of the present PRO site and organization.

COHORT STUDIES

Cohort studies have been recognized as one of the best devices (expensive but irreplaceable) for following biological and social development through a considerable part of the human life-span.

There has not so far as we know been any attempt anywhere in the world to include questions relating to the polity in a cohort study, and it would be regrettable if an opportunity were lost. The possible questions can be very broadly phrased, and need not involve any reference to party affiliation of a kind which would cause offence: the main problems are perhaps those of leadership, conformity, and information regarding issues which involve social integration and social decision-making.

COMPUTER FACILITIES

So far, the number of British political scientists who use computers is quite small, and none of them has complained about difficulties of access. They do, however, have difficulties, of a kind common to the social sciences, in keeping abreast of the rapid development of computer techniques; and there is a need for skilled intermediaries, computer experts specializing in analysis for the social sciences.

Research overseas

The individual and general facilities so far discussed are relevant primarily to research in British institutions, but it would be a mistake to give too much emphasis to research in this country. Such research is essential: but there is a sense in which all political science is comparative, in that institutions can be specified only by comparative analysis, and the most

61

powerful tool of analysis is that of international comparison, guided by intellectual discipline.

Work outside Britain is essential to political science as a discipline; all degrees in politics include work on comparative government, under one title or another, and such teaching cannot flourish without research. Understanding of politics now requires understanding of its world context.

This is essentially an intellectual problem; but it is related to problems of cultural influence and dependence. Rather late, but with great vigour, American scholars have entered the field of comparative studies, and their publications are on the way to domination of the academic market. In so far as their analysis is good, this investment is of value to British scholars; but even the best American work reflects American preoccupations, and it is important that British political scientists should be able to utilize it without being dominated by it. British contributions to the study of comparative politics have been distinguished; but there is a risk that UK research may now tend to flow along the lines which are most convenient and least costly: in general, towards political theory in some form, towards contemporary history (British and international) and towards observation of British practice. This is, up to a point, admirable: but some positive action may be required to encourage British initiative in the study of countries other than the UK.

Competence in the comparative study of society requires first that a man be trained by disciplined research in the institutions of a society other than his own. This requires fieldwork, which falls into three different categories.

First, there is work in English-speaking countries, above all in the USA. American affluence and generosity make it possible for any good British graduate to work in an American university for two or three years. This is almost always valuable educationally; but it is rather apt to distract attention from the possibility of work in the English-speaking countries associated with the Commonwealth. A fair number go to Canada; a few to Australia; virtually none to New Zealand, Ireland, or South Africa, all countries of great interest to students of politics.

As for more senior research workers, it is not easy to find exceptions to the bald proposition that no important research has been carried out in recent years by any scholar based on an English university in any of the English-speaking 'countries of settlement'. Possible exceptions might be in the comparative study of federalism, and of the institutions of the Commonwealth.

Second, there is research in Europe, West and East, including research into supra-national institutions. Costs of travel and maintenance are less than in English-speaking countries overseas, but other difficulties are greater. The traditions of these countries in political science are different from that of Britain, so that interchange is more difficult; and English diffidence about foreign languages means that not many qualified students come forward. What has been achieved in this field by British political scientists is of real importance, perhaps more important than the work they have published about English-speaking countries in recent years: but it is not easy to sustain and develop research of this kind. A long-term effort is required, and this may involve support for programmes as well as for projects, including programmes for collaboration with European universities.

Third, the 'non-Western world' admits of no generalizations and has to serve here as residual category. British political scientists have initial advantages derived from the period of imperial access and experience, and these advantages can to some extent be retained through continuing arrangements with what were once 'colonial' universities (and some of these are still being created) from Fiji and Hong

Kong round the world westward to Jamaica, Trinidad, and Guyana. There are various liaison arrangements sponsored by the Ministry for Overseas Development and other organizations which on the whole work well; but large-scale research support is outside their scope, and may not flourish unless backed by the SSRC.

These old imperial connections will fade if not sustained; and there are important areas in which they do not exist, in particular Latin America. It is obvious that there cannot be strong, UK-based research programmes in all the developing countries, but opportunities for political research are especially vulnerable to political crises, and there is much to be said for dispersal rather than concentration. If there were a policy of concentrating development research in specific areas, it would make possible substantial programmes, but they would be continually at risk. In this field, therefore, the policy of backing individual initiative should on the whole be adhered to, if the plan is good and the political climate is tolerably favourable. This will of course involve commitment to the cost of fieldwork in the same way as for social anthropologists.